Ransomware: Prevention and Recovery

Ransomware: Prevention and Recovery

How to Avoid Paying a Ransom

DAVID C. PETTIT

Copyright © 2017 by David C. Pettit

All rights reserved. No part of this publication may be reproduced in any form or by any means, including scanning, photocopying, or otherwise without prior written permission of the copyright holder.

ISBN-10: 154827660X
ISBN-13: 978-1548276607

First Printing, 2017

Printed in the United States of America

43 | 9781548276607 | **43**

WH: Aisle 16 Row: Bay 1
Bay: Shelf 4

ZBM.4MN2

Title:	Ransomware - Prevention and Recovery: How to Avoid Paying a Ransom
Cond:	Very Good
User:	bc_lister3
Station:	Lister-03
Date:	2024-11-19 18:57:11 (UTC)
Account:	Zoom Books Company
Orig Loc:	Aisle 16-Bay 1-Shelf 4
mSKU:	ZBM.4MN2
vSKU:	ZBV.154827660X.VG
Seq#:	43
unit_id:	20866054
width:	0.39 in
rank:	6,279,373

ZBV.154827660X.VG

delist unit# 20866054

xxxxx

DEDICATION

In gratitude to our faithful clients, my two sons (IT professionals who assist me as much as I assist them), my wife who encourages me in my writing endeavors, and those who have hired me in various roles in the information technology industry spanning over 34 years

PREFACE

In early 2017 I found out that a client of mine had suffered a ransomware disaster before choosing my company for information technology services. Little wonder why that company made a switch. Someone let them down. With ransomware all over the technology industry news and the advent of the WannaCryptor (WannaCry for short) variant harming thousands of companies and making national news, I thought it time to write a book for my clients and prospects so that we could together prevent or at least minimize the impact of an attack and recover effectively in little time and for little cost rather than pay a ransom and suffer the reputation hit that comes with doing so. While doing research, I found a absence of books of any quality – just one of any significant value. In past decades I have written a number of white papers and some network documentation on technical matters. I have gathered and created many information technology Standards, Policies, Procedures, and Checklists. Even the decent ransomware book that I found lacked most of these. And I have had over a decade of full-time backup and disaster recovery experience, preventing disasters for hundreds of company clients. The time seemed right. This book is the result of information technology experience, technical writing experience, and current events.

DAVID C. PETTIT

TIGARD, OREGON, USA

06-20-2017

ACKNOWLEDGMENTS

My thanks goes out to my two sons, Michael and Matthew Pettit, for their review of this book. Both are IT professionals who have dealt directly with one or more ransomware attacks upon one or more businesses. I thank Timothy Phillips for his excellent proofreading. And I thank my wife Kelley for her perspective on this book. All the input has been valuable.

INTRODUCTION

Because a successful and complete ransomware attack could cripple your business, harm its reputation, and even cause its failure, you need to know the content of this book and take the action steps suggested. You will find essential information, case studies, and suggested action steps. Those include risk assessment, assignment of roles, creating documents, and implementing best practices for both prevention and for recovery. When used well, some of those things can help ensure the continuity of your business by having an adequate disaster recovery plan for a ransomware attack.

CONTENTS

DEDICATION v

PREFACE vii

ACKNOWLEDGMENTS ix

INTRODUCTION xi

1 Ransomware Defined 1

2 Ransomware - Is It Real? 5

3 Ransomware Infection Methods 9

4 Ransomware Prevalence – Is it Only on Windows Computers? 15

5 Ransomware Variants 25

6 How Ransomware Works 29

7 Ransomware Prevention 33

8 The Technical Part of Ransomware Prevention 45

9 Learn of and Perform Security Updates Immediately 55

10 The User Education Part of Ransomware Prevention and recovery 59

11 Recovery from a Ransomware Attack 69

12 Virtual Machines for Ransomware Recovery 71

13 The Backup Part of Ransomware Prevention and Recovery 77

14 The Business End of Ransomware Prevention and Recovery 81

15 About Paying a Ransom 85

16 Managed Security Services 91

17 Actionable Items 97

18 Security Alert Suggestions 101

19 Ransomware Standards 107

20 Ransomware Policies 109

21 Ransomware Procedures 113

22 Ransomware Checklists 117

23 Ransomware Forms 125

24 Your Worksheets 129

EPILOGUE 149

ABOUT THE AUTHOR 151

ENGAGEMENTS 153

1 RANSOMWARE DEFINED

Ransomware can encrypt computer files until a ransom is paid to unlock them, and may include not only the encryption of user-generated data files but may include server or workstation operating system files such that the server or computer is rendered non-functional. Well, the criminal will leave it functional enough to display of the ransom note and accept the entry and use of the decryption key once the ransom is paid.

Ransomware: Prevention and Recovery

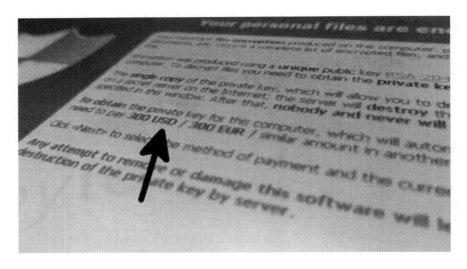

The last part of that is a best case scenario. Some ransomware has been so poor that it fails in its decryption effort, leaving the infected system and files useless in spite of a ransom having been paid and decryption key having been provided. Some ransomware has introduced a timer such that, once a deadline has passed, payment and a decryption key no longer help. Such timeframes have been as little as six hours.

From https://en.wikipedia.org/wiki/Ransomware
06-12-2017

> While some simple ransomware may lock the system in a way which is not difficult for a

knowledgeable person to reverse, more advanced malware uses a technique called cryptoviral extortion, in which it encrypts the victim's files, making them inaccessible, and demands a ransom payment to decrypt them. In a properly implemented cryptoviral extortion attack, recovering the files without the decryption key is an intractable problem - and difficult to trace digital currencies such as Ukash and Bitcoin are used for the ransoms, making tracing and prosecuting the perpetrators difficult.

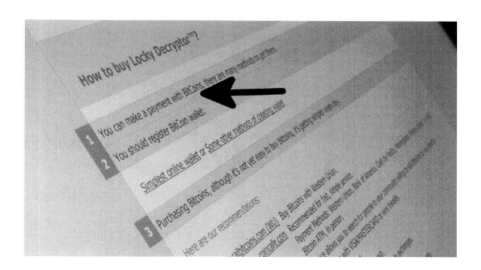

Ransomware: Prevention and Recovery

2 RANSOMWARE - IS IT REAL?

In an article on Security InfoWatch dated 06-12-2017, we see that it is more real than ever, making big leaps in 2016 and 2017.

From http://www.securityinfowatch.com/article/12337355/ransomware-the-risk-is-real 06-13-2017

Ransomware: The Risk is Real

On May 12, the now-familiar threat of ransomware took the offensive, as more than 230,000 computers in 150 countries were encrypted for ransom at hospitals, telecommunications systems, governments, banks and more.

From https://www.theguardian.com/technology/2017/may/12/nhs-ransomware-cyber-attack-what-is-wanacrypt0r-20 06-13-2017

WannaCry is asking for $300 worth of the cryptocurrency Bitcoin to unlock the contents of the computers. . . .

Cyber threats and ransomware in particular is one of the most talked about topics among the security community today. Ransomware presents a major threat across all businesses and vertical markets. Much of the ransomware is coming from out-of-country hackers who are quite adept in their attacks, often demanding bitcoin as payment. . . .

Online extortion had a banner year in 2016, according to Trend Micro's annual security assessment report: "2016 Security Roundup: A Record

Year for Enterprise Threats." In 2016 there was a 752 percent increase in new ransomware families . . .

Trend Micro has a February 28, 2017 article with a graph of the increase.

From https://www.trendmicro.com/vinfo/us/security/research-and-analysis/threat-reports/roundup

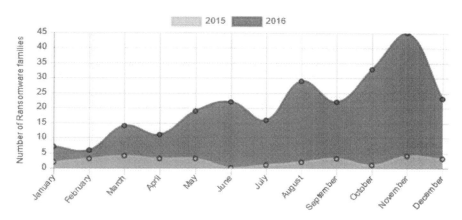

Ransomware attacks are growing in frequency, causing devastating consequences to enterprises and organizations across the globe.

Ransomware: Prevention and Recovery

3 RANSOMWARE INFECTION METHODS

Methods by which a ransomware infection happens vary. Some is by user action. Some takes place even without user activity.

From https://en.wikipedia.org/wiki/Ransomware 06-12-2017

> Ransomware attacks are typically carried out using a Trojan that is disguised as a legitimate file that the user is tricked into downloading, or opening when it arrives as an email attachment. However, one high profile example, the "WannaCry worm", traveled

Ransomware: Prevention and Recovery

automatically between computers without user interaction.

From http://blog.emsisoft.com/2017/03/30/spotlight-on-ransomware-common-infection-methods/ 06-13-2017

> Spotlight on Ransomware: Common infection methods
>
> Malware writers and attackers use a variety of sophisticated techniques to spread their malware. There are three commonly used ransomware infection methods that will be explored in this post; malicious email attachments and links, drive-by downloads and Remote Desktop Protocol attacks.

From https://heimdalsecurity.com/blog/what-is-ransomware-protection 06-13-2017

> Nevertheless, these are the most common infection methods used by cybercriminals
>
> - Spam email campaigns that contain malicious links or attachments (there are plenty

of forms that malware can use for disguise on the web);
- Security exploits in vulnerable software;
- Internet traffic redirects to malicious websites;
- Legitimate websites that have malicious code injected in their web pages;
- Drive-by downloads;
- Malvertising campaigns;
- SMS messages (when targeting mobile devices);
- Botnets;
- Self-propagation (spreading from one infected computer to another); WannaCry, for instance, used an exploit kit that scanned a user's PC, looking for a certain vulnerability, and then launched a ransomware attack that targeted it.
- Affiliate schemes in ransomware-as-a-service. Basically, the developer behind the ransomware earns a cut of the profits each time a user pays the ransom.

These attacks get more refined by the day, as cyber criminals learn from their mistakes and tweak their malicious code to be stronger, more intrusive and better suited to avoid cyber security solutions. The WannaCry attack is a perfect example of this since it used a wide-spread Windows vulnerability to infect a computer with basically no user interaction.

As you can see, user education and being careful, though essential as part of prevention, is not enough.

4 RANSOMWARE PREVALENCE – IS IT ONLY ON WINDOWS COMPUTERS?

Microsoft Windows systems are not the only targets and systems of victims. Apple, Linux, and even mobile smart phones are the subjects of ransomware attacks.

From https://en.wikipedia.org/wiki/Ransomware
06-12-2017

> Different tactics have been used on iOS devices, such as exploiting iCloud accounts and using the Find My iPhone system to lock access to the device. On iOS 10.3, Apple patched a bug in the handling of

Ransomware: Prevention and Recovery

JavaScript pop-up windows in Safari that had been exploited by ransomware websites.

In three articles about ransomware infections on Apple Mac systems, we see that Macs are very much targets.

From http://www.bbc.com/news/technology-40261693 06-13-2017

Apple Mac computers targeted by ransomware and spyware

Mac users are being warned about new variants of malware that have been created specifically to target

Apple computers.

. . .

In its analysis, AlienVault researcher Peter Ewane said the malicious code in the spyware tried hard to evade many of the standard ways security programs spot and stop such programs.

Mr. Ewane said Mac users needed to start being more vigilant as malware creators targeted them.

"As OS X continues to grow in market share we can expect malware authors to invest greater amounts of time in producing malware for this platform."

From https://www.laptopmag.com/articles/mac-ransomware-spyware 06-13-2017

Macs Face Double Threat from New Ransomware, Spyware

A new strain of Mac ransomware will encrypt files on your Mac's hard drive and demand that you pay about $700 to (maybe) get them back. A strain of Mac spyware created by the same author aims to capture screenshots, ambient audio, user photos and browser history from compromised Macs.

From https://www.theinquirer.net/inquirer/news/3011819/macransom-ransomware-as-a-service-is-now-targeting-macos-users-too 06-13-2017

MacRansom: Ransomware-as-a-service is now targeting macOS users too

SECURITY RESEARCHERS have found the first evidence of ransomware-as-a-service (RaaS) affecting Apple machines, dubbed 'MacRansom.'

It is pretty clear that Apple Mac systems are vulnerable to ransomware attack and that there

are those who are targeting them. In fact, in one way it is worse – the recent ransom request for Mac units was $700 while the recent ransom request for Windows units was $300.

Linux systems are not left out. I mention this because, historically, many technology pundits have been down on Microsoft as THE vulnerable platform with the implication that Apple and Linux platforms are not vulnerable. Ransomware criminals are not as picky as other malware creators may have been in the past. They are equal opportunity thieves.

From http://techworldblog.in/hackers-now-exploiting-sambacry-vulnerability-attack-linux/?utm_source=hs_email&utm_medium=email&utm_content=53525713&_hsenc=p2ANqtz-9bcnAofg0YfWKpAPdBGp8-olGk847s7Hh7KVuNZa_WCYWJH5u37pC9_4AVbWsmRqmxtJCPCL8-DMOnWFv_9bNB2OAWtMyzGikeREFOYvoZGldogAE&_hsmi=53525713 06-24-2017

> Hackers now exploiting SambaCry vulnerability to attack Linux!
>
> SambaCry is using a vulnerability in Samba installations to compromise Linux machines and use them as victims in a large cryptocurrency (Bitcoin or Monero or any other currency) mining process, also enables a remote attacker to hack into affected Linux

systems.

Samba said in a security advisory:

All versions of Samba from 3.5.0 onwards are vulnerable to a remote code execution vulnerability, allowing a malicious client to upload a shared library to a writable share, and then cause the server to load and execute it.

SambaCry can be simply exploited under specific situations . . .

. . .

If these situations are met, remote hackers can upload any code of their choosing and cause the server to execute it, possibly with unfettered root privileges, depending on the vulnerable platform.

Linux systems need to be kept up to date just like Windows systems do, especially right after discovery of malware becoming "active in the wild" on them.

Android smartphones are vulnerable too. Keep them updated as soon as a notification of an update comes in.

From http://www.guidingtech.com/67358/wannacry-ransomware-android-vulnerabilities-unsafe/ 06-24-2017

> WannaCry Ransomware: Are Smartphones Safe? Is the Danger Still Looming?
>
> The good news is Google releases security updates for Android devices almost every month — although in certain countries the carriers are responsible for rolling these over to their customers.
>
> . . .
>
> Although there isn't much to worry about, a flaw was recently discovered by security experts which remain unfixed by Google and can lead to a ransomware attack on Android devices. The flaw will only be fixed in Google's next

David C. Pettit

OS update — Android 'O'.

It seems that smartphones are targets, and updates need to be applied as soon as they are made available.

Ransomware: Prevention and Recovery

5 RANSOMWARE VARIANTS

There are a number of ransomware variants: Spora, Cerber, Osiris, Goldeneye Petya, Wallet Dharma, TeslaCrypt, CryptXXX, CryptoWall, Locky, and Ranscam. They can have one or both of two effects – 1) encrypt user generated content – such as your files – and 2) render a computer useless (for the time being) except for ransom notices and a way to pay the ransom. A brief introduction to them shows that there are various means of delivery and differing levels of infection.

From https://en.wikipedia.org/wiki/Locky 06-12-2017

Locky is ransomware malware released in 2016. It is delivered by email (that was allegedly an invoice requiring payment) with an attached Microsoft Word document that contains malicious macros.

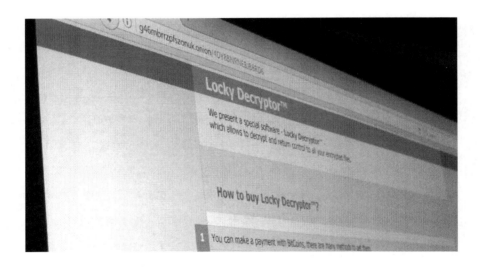

That attack is one reason many information technology professionals have disabled the macros function in Word for users who do not need that function.

From https://en.wikipedia.org/wiki/TeslaCrypt 06-12-2017

TeslaCrypt was a ransomware Trojan. It is now defunct, and its master key released by the developers. A free decryption tool is available on the web.

In its early forms, TeslaCrypt targeted game-play data for specific computer games. Newer variants of the malware also affect other file types.

From https://en.wikipedia.org/wiki/CryptoLocker 06-12-2017

The CryptoLocker ransomware attack was a cyberattack using the CryptoLocker ransomware that occurred from 5 September 2013 to late-May 2014. The attack utilized a Trojan that targeted computers running Microsoft Windows, and was believed to have first been posted to the Internet on 5 September 2013. It propagated via infected email attachments, and via an existing botnet; when activated, the malware encrypts certain types of files stored on local and mounted network drives . . .

That last part is worth special note. Since ransomware – and other malware – can affect mounted network drives, you need to know that an infection of just one computer or server can affect files in many locations, not just files on that one computer or server. That is why offline backups are essential.

6 HOW RANSOMWARE WORKS

In the book "Ransomware: Defending Against Digital Extortion," authors Allan Liska and Timothy Gallo give us the "anatomy of a ransomware attack": Deployment, Installation, Command-and-Control, Destruction, Extortion. They add that the average ransom for 2016 is about $300, some Mac versions have been for about $700, and some attacks on corporations request many thousands of dollars. But that is just part of the trouble. Payment may not get you back your files or system in working order, and a reoccurrence can happen. They suggest not paying a ransom in most cases. See Chapter 14 for a quote on the topic.

Ransomware: Prevention and Recovery

Sophos has a similar list, in five stages, with some explanations of each.

From https://news.sophos.com/en-us/2015/03/03/anatomy-of-a-ransomware-attack-cryptolocker-cryptowall-and-how-to-stay-safe-infographic 06-13-2017

> Anatomy of a ransomware attack: CryptoLocker, CryptoWall, and how to stay safe (Infographic)
>
> 1. Installation – after a victim's computer is infected, the crypto-ransomware installs itself, and sets keys in the Windows Registry to start automatically every time your computer boots up.
> 2. Contacting Headquarters – Before crypto-ransomware can attack you, it contacts a server operated by the criminal gang that owns it.
> 3. Handshake and Keys – The ransomware client and server identify each other through a carefully arranged "handshake," and the server generates two

cryptographic keys. One key is kept on your computer, the second key is stored securely on the criminals' server.
4. Encryption – With the cryptographic keys established, the ransomware on your computer starts encrypting every file it finds with any of dozens of common file extensions, from Microsoft Office documents to .JPG images and more.
5. Extortion – The ransomware displays a screen giving you a time limit to pay up before the criminals destroy the key to decrypt your files. The typical price, $300 to $500, must be paid in untraceable bitcoins or other electronic payments.

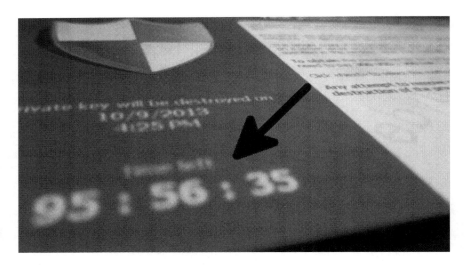

You'll have to excuse some of the writing above. They are not my words. To be true to the citation, the words are given as provided in the original infographic. In spite of that, the stages of a ransomware attack are valid.

7 RANSOMWARE PREVENTION

You can avoid paying a ransom to unlock (decrypt) your computer files by prevention and or preparation. The quick summary of proper computing practices that enables you to avoid becoming a victim of ransomware is to 1) utilize known multiple methods of prevention, 2) utilizing multiple ways of not having to rely solely on the current computers and current active files on the computers at your business, 3) not relying on backups that remain network connected all the time, and 4) not relying on just 7 to 30 days of backup versions.

Before we get too far and you bail on this book because you know you have backup, let me give some fair warning. Ransomware commonly looks for, finds, and encrypts the backup as well as the original files. See page 44, the file types targeted. Oops! So we can't afford to get too cocky about your backup and recovery strategy.

In addition to adequate backup, a qualified professional should be engaged to plan your protection, response, and recovery. Consider this: You use all of this thorough book (and perhaps more material) and implement all suggestions and test that it all will work. Then, a year from now (or less), the criminals adapt and ramp up the attack to a new level. That level, which will surely come, involves introducing a rolling encryption strategy that looks at the "last modified" date of files and also uses an algorithm that encrypts some pre-determined types and names of files some months, other files some weeks, and yet more files just days before revealing the ransom notice, then the rest on the reveal date. In this scenario, it is likely that every backup version for some or most of the files going back in time is also compromised, quite possibly including critical and needed files. Oops! Someone who knows what they are doing needs to be in charge of your plan and its implementation. Someone who knows or anticipates the next attack method.

The above scenario is quite plausible. In an article titled "Ransomware attacks are becoming more sophisticated" it is clear that criminals are advancing their sophistication.

From https://betanews.com/2017/06/13/ransomware-increasing-sophistication 06-13-2017

> Ransomware attacks are becoming more sophisticated
>
> As one of the world's leading cyber-security companies, Sophos is able to track habits and trends across the globe, and has noted that criminals are becoming ever

more sophisticated when it comes to ransomware.

. . .

Speaking to ITProPortal this week, the company's (Sophos') senior security researcher James Lyne stated: "However, as criminals become more professional and business-like, the potential threat to consumers and businesses will continue to grow, so the need to increase research and protection levels is now."

Ransomware code is being sold as a commodity, making it widely available to "professional" coders to customize:

From the same source:

> "It's a business, but there's something in this new professionalism that is crossing the technical to business boundary...and they are getting better," Lyne warns.

And there is evidence that ransomware can and does selectively target particular file types:

From https://en.wikipedia.org/wiki/TeslaCrypt 06-12-2017

> In its original, game-player campaign, upon infection the malware searched for 185 file extensions related to 40 different games . . .

. . .

Lyne explained that malware packets are being sold on online marketplaces, allowing criminals to personalize their own attacks, with some even featuring marketing videos to show off their wares.

A well-respected source of protection and information, Malwarebytes, has an article called "Explained: Spora ransomware." In it is a very detailed explanation of what the Spora ransomware does.

From https://blog.malwarebytes.com/threat-analysis/2017/03/spora-ransomware 06-13-2017

After being deployed, Spora ransomware runs silently and encrypts files with selected extensions. Then, it attempts to redeploy itself with elevated privileges. No UAC bypass mechanism has been used – instead, the UAC popup appears repeatedly till the user accepts it:

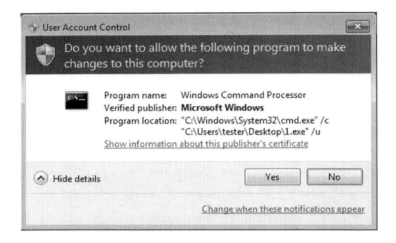

and

Explained: Spora ransomware

. . .

What is attacked?

Spora ransomware attacks the following extensions:

      xls doc xlsx docx rtf odt pdf psd dwg

cdr cd mdb 1cd dbf sqlite accdb jpg

jpeg tiff zip rar 7z backup sql bak

They are grouped in several categories, used to build statistics for the attackers. The categories can be described as such: office documents, PDF/PPT documents, Corel Draw documents, database files, images, and archives . . .

A note for those who do not know what some of those extensions are for. The first few are for common user documents: Excel spreadsheets, Word documents, Adobe PDF files. MDB, DBF and SQL types are for databases built with user data entry. RAR and BAK are used for common for backup files. ZIP and 7Z are used for archive files. Spora ransomware targets them all – originals, archives, and backups. And the archived and backed up files may include many other original file types than those listed. Nasty!

From https://blog.malwarebytes.com/threat-analysis/2017/03/spora-ransomware 06-13-2017

Explained: Spora ransomware

While there currently is no decryption for those infected we suggest keeping a backup of the infected files as there might be a decrypter in the future.

The reason for that suggestion is that in the past there have been decryption solutions for a

number of ransomware attacks:

From https://heimdalsecurity.com/blog/what-is-ransomware-protection 06-13-2017

> Cyber security experts managed to find flaws in TeslaCrypt's encryption algorithm twice. They created decryption tools and did their best so that the malware creators wouldn't find out.
>
> ESET researchers managed to get the universal master decryption key from them and built a decrypter that you can use if you happen to be a victim of TeslaCrypt.

From https://heimdalsecurity.com/blog/what-is-ransomware-protection 06-13-2017

> What is Ransomware and 15 Easy Steps To Keep Your System Protected [Updated]
>
> . . .

It has the ability to remain dormant – the ransomware can remain inactive on the system until the computer is at its most vulnerable moment and take advantage of that to strike fast and effectively.

Ransomware prevention needs to involve a multi-pronged approach. There are technical steps to be taken by those in charge of company information technology (IT) staff and the company information security vendor. IT staff should have information security training. User education about ransomware and other malware can help a lot, and is useful for both prevention and for notifying IT staff of an event or suspected attempt. A virtual machines environment can help tremendously with fast and full recovery. Adequate backup must be of an appropriate type, be performed constantly, and be configured from a mitigation perspective. Business perspective must be considered, including cost/benefit analysis. Each of these is worthy of its own chapter.

8 THE TECHNICAL PART OF RANSOMWARE PREVENTION

Although the following article starts out defining ransomware and giving examples by name and effect, it ends with very helpful advice. Here is some of it:

From http://www.gfi.com/blog/how-to-protect-against-ransomware-in-three-easy-steps/ 11-14-2016

How to protect against ransomware in three easy steps

1. Scan all emails and web downloads with at least two antivirus engines

   This ensures that the initial infection has a much lower chance of propagating over the corporate network. Multiple antivirus engines help to mitigate zero-day threats and increase the likelihood that the malware is identified and stopped before it enters the network.

2. Block user access to malicious or vulnerable websites

   Apart from email, ransomware can propagate itself via malicious and vulnerable websites. Vulnerable websites are a major concern because they are legitimate websites that users trust and use regularly. However, these sites can be used as an accessory for a ransomware infection because the attackers will have exploited vulnerabilities, like XSS, to execute code on the user's machine, and instruct the browser to download the malicious payload. The ability to prevent user access to trustworthy, but vulnerable, websites as well as dangerous, malicious websites greatly lowers the risk of a ransomware infection.

3. Monitor and block outbound connections to TOR / anonymity networks

   If a ransomware infection occurs, in spite of advanced perimeter antivirus protection, having the capability to monitor web traffic will help to identify the infection and its source. Furthermore, the capability to automatically block traffic to anonymity networks, used by the ransomware to get the encryption keys, will prevent the malware from applying strong file encryption. Without an encryption key, the malware will not work, the infection will not be registered thus preventing the attackers from knowing if the malware infiltrated the corporate network or (and therefore launch other attacks on) the corporate network.

These are important steps to take however it is impossible to monitor traffic manually 24/7. Automation is a sysadmin's much-loved word.

Those points require some evaluation. Regarding point 1, if one uses the best of the best antivirus software that has constant updates and has a reputation of being among the fastest at updating when a zero day threat takes place, and if the computers using it are left on and "awake" (i.e. not in sleep, hibernate, or standby mode any more than necessary) so that the updates can occur in the fastest possible timeframe, one antivirus software may be adequate (in my experienced opinion). One thing missing from the article is that antivirus engines

need to be on servers, workstations, and perimeter devices such as firewalls. Routers need to have a great set of rules about the what is allowed past them. Best practice is defense at all points, not just on user workstations (end-points), not on just firewalls (the perimeter), and not just on servers.

Regarding point 2, more needs to be explained. To accomplish what it says, one needs the kind of security software that is always on and watching user activity and that provides what is called "endpoint security." That is a level of protection that goes beyond detecting – that includes monitoring activity and websites accessed. And it must not only detect and monitor viruses but also other types of malware. The point I am making is that it is not enough to just have anti-virus software on the computer. In addition, the point the writer made of "preventing user access" stops short. It fails to cover some of the means of prevention. Besides software protection, there are computer settings that can be made, such as disabling Internet browsers for those who do not need Internet access, limiting user profiles to user vs. administrator level privileges to prevent installation of malware if it reaches the computer, and more. These are the kinds of things a well-qualified security-conscious computer technician does.

Regarding point 3, an indispensable part of monitoring is logging what takes place. That gives technical staff the ability to identify and thereby more likely succeed at blocking future attacks by the same source. Be sure that your chosen protection suite includes logging and quickly getting those logs to reputable security vendors such as your anti-virus and anti-malware provider.

It's one thing to scan, another to monitor, log, and report, but what matters most is having the ability to continue business operations even if the worst thing happens on a computer (when I say computer, I include those that fall in the category of server and all of the variety of servers that exist, such as file servers, database servers, and application servers, to name just three). Before I get to the next article, let me give my take. There are five things necessary to ensure business continuity in such a worst case: 1) Alternate computers and/or servers need to be readily available since the ransomware may have not only encrypted files but also render the entire hardware device useless. That is the hardware part. 2) Archived copies of all in-use software needs to be readily at hand for installation on the replacement hardware. Any needed activation keys need to be available with the software. 3) Proven ability to restore company data files from backup to a replacement computer or server. Periodic restore of files can prove the ability to restore from backup. 4) Proven documentation and procedures, preferably with checklists, for how to make the replacement hardware, installed software, and restored data work again the way it must for company operations to resume within an acceptable timeframe. 5) Appropriate staff who can implement the recovery that uses the first four things.

In a document available for download on Datto's website is an explanation of why just protection is not enough:

> RansomwareGuide.pdf
>
> Ransomware is distributed in a variety of ways and is difficult to protect against because, just like

the flu virus, it is constantly evolving.

Because ransomware is from time to time different than what protection software knows, it is therefore undetectable and free to infect and encrypt systems and data until its characteristics are identified and the protection catches up to it through an update. In summary, one cannot assume that having protective anti-virus and anti-malware software is all that you need, even if it is on all systems from perimeter to end-point.

In addition, as ransomware morphs, so must user education. Training material and presentations must be kept up to date or it may become useless.

9 LEARN OF AND PERFORM SECURITY UPDATES IMMEDIATELY

update

Since ransomware and other malware attacks take advantage of operating system vulnerabilities, operating system vendors (think Microsoft for its Windows products and Apple for its Mac products) frequently update their software with versions and parts that "plug the holes," so to speak, and make those updates available to customers. There once was a day when we IT professionals suggested waiting about six months before applying updates so that any newly introduced bugs could be discovered by other "guinea pigs" and then be patched before we suffered the same indignity of updating and then experiencing trouble. But, when malware became so prevalent a few years ago, the tradeoff of staying vulnerable vs. avoiding new software bugs became unacceptable. Now we always recommend keeping systems up to date as soon as updates are made available. Be sure to update 1) the operating system (Windows, Linux, macOS), 2) software (QuickBooks, Microsoft Office, etc.) and 3) anti-virus databases and definitions. The latter, anti-virus databases, should be updated at least daily. Most do so automatically. But make sure it is happening.

Some attacks happen the same day that a vulnerability is discovered and announced. That is called a "zero-day attack." And, yes, there are those who announce vulnerabilities as soon as discovered. That brings up a whole other argument about whether it is best to announce them immediately or not, but we won't address that topic. Regardless, make sure you or your responsible IT staff or service company is subscribed to good security alerts. See the end matter of this book for some suggestions. When an alert comes out, make sure that suggested updates are performed immediately.

Ransomware: Prevention and Recovery

10 THE USER EDUCATION PART OF RANSOMWARE PREVENTION AND RECOVERY

The next article covers some of what the prior one in Chapter 8 missed entirely. It speaks only to the technology part of prevention. The next one mentions another very important aspect of prevention, that of user education.

From http://www.datto.com/blog/how-to-protect-against-ransomware 11-14-2016

How To Protect Against Ransomware

. . . A proper ransomware protection strategy requires a

three-pronged approach, comprising of education, security and backup.

- **Education:** First and foremost, education is essential to protect your business against ransomware. It is critical that your staff understands what ransomware is and the threats that it poses. Provide your team with specific examples of suspicious emails with clear instructions on what to do if they encounter a potential ransomware lure (i.e. don't open attachments, if you see something, say something, etc.). Conduct bi-annual formal training to inform staff about the risk of ransomware and other cyber threats. When new employees join the team, make sure you send them an email to bring them up to date about cyber best practices. It is important to ensure that the message is communicated clearly to everyone in the organization, not passed around on a word of mouth basis.

Lastly, keep staff updated as new ransomware enters the market or changes over time.
- **Security:** Antivirus software should be considered essential for any business to protect against ransomware and other risks. Ensure your security software is up to date, as well, in order to protect against newly identified threats. Keep all business applications patched and updated in order to minimize vulnerabilities. Some antivirus software products offer ransomware-specific functionality. Sophos, for example, offers technology that monitors systems to detect malicious activities such as file extension or registry changes. If ransomware is detected, the software has the ability to block it and alert users. However, because ransomware is constantly evolving, even the best security software can be breached. This is why a secondary layer of defense is critical for businesses to ensure

recovery in case malware strikes: backup.

- **Backup:** Modern total data protection solutions, like Datto, take snapshot-based, incremental backups as frequently as every five minutes to create a series of recovery contacts. If your business suffers a ransomware attack, this technology allows you to roll back your data to a point-in-time before the corruption occurred. When it comes to ransomware, the benefit of this is two-fold. First, you don't need to pay the ransom to get your data back. Second, since you are restoring to a point-in-time before the ransomware infected your systems, you can be certain everything is clean and the malware can not be triggered again. . . .

Additionally, some data protection products today allow users to run applications from image-based backups of virtual machines. This capability is commonly referred to as "recovery-in-place" or "instant recovery." This technology can be useful for recovering from a ransomware attack as well because it allows you to continue operations while your primary systems are being restored and with little to no downtime. Datto's version of this business saving technology is called Instant Virtualization, which virtualizes systems either locally or remotely in a secure cloud within seconds. This solution ensures businesses stay up and running when disaster strikes.

As always, taking the proper precautions is the best way to protect yourself from any form of ransomware. In the event you're attacked, the best way to avoid paying a ransom is to have a proper business continuity and disaster recovery (BCDR) solution featuring up-to-date backups. This will allow you to restore your data to a point in time before the infection, and retain your precious data.

Although very good, including the correct three-pronged approach, the above article missed some things you must know. Let me add them here. Even after recovery to a point in time before an infection, contrary to what the article says, such recovery does not in and of itself prevent a recurrence of the infection. If one just does the same things again, the infection will take place again. A great time for user education, a refresh of best practices, is at the time of infection and recovery. In addition, discovery of the cause of the infection, from logs and more, can pinpoint the activity that enabled the infection and then staff can be instructed to avoid such activity and technicians can implement measures, if any exist, to technically prevent a recurrence.

In a downloadable PDF file named EBK_Ransomware_SMB_Final.pdf, the article "Intronis MSP Solutions by Barracuda," the writer agrees with the need for employee education:

In order to protect your organization from cyber threats, you need to keep ransomware and cybersecurity top-of-mind and educate your employees about this destructive type of malware and the damage it can do to your business.

Good point. But it lacks in usable detail. At a minimum you need to know what to teach and plan how often to provide education. When you do your research into training materials, you'll find them mostly under the term "security awareness training." With materials you get from a company that keeps them up to date, there is no need to create the material from scratch. If you purchase the materials, you avoid any accusation of plagiarism.

One method of teaching is group presentations. Have them. But they are not enough. During them, introduce the other training methods that your company will employ.

David C. Pettit

One additional method I like is one that makes more and lasting impact and is more realistic than showing slides and providing handouts. A simulator with which an employee interacts is my favorite method. One example is the anti-phishing simulator called SecurityIQ by Infosec Institute. It does a good job. One reason is that it is a fun challenge, unlike everything else that employees will find to be dry subject matter. Remember the fact that retention is better if someone writes, which is better than if someone sees, which is better than if someone hears information. The same concept here – clicks on a simulator will have employees retain security awareness training points better than seeing handouts and better than hearing a presentation. As of 2017-03-13, the mentioned simulator can be found at https://securityiq.infosecinstitute.com/?resources-sidebar?resources-sidebar

11 RECOVERY FROM A RANSOMWARE ATTACK

Since ransomware can affect both computer functionality and files with user generated content, a business needs to be able to 1) "flatten" a computer – in essence make it as if it just came off the manufacturing line, reinstall an operating system such as Windows, reinstall application software such as Office 2016, QuickBooks, and other line-of-business software such as OpenEMR, and 2) restore backed up files. Depending upon the original "environment," the time to recover can vary widely. If a computer is what is called a "virtual machine," recovery of the computer (not counting the user files) can be very fast, typically under 15 minutes. If a computer is "imaged" regularly, recovery can be fairly fast, typically under an hour. But if file backup and restore is the only part of the plan, the flattening and rebuilding part of the recovery can take a long time, typically hours. Let's look at recovering from ransomware when there is a virtual machine environment.

12 VIRTUAL MACHINES FOR RANSOMWARE RECOVERY

Virtual machines refer to a server or workstation that exists in a file image that is loaded into memory on another usually "beefier" computer, typically a server, which most often hosts multiple virtual machines at the same time. By "loaded into memory," what I mean is that the operating system (Windows, Linux, etc.) and configuration settings are not installed onto a computer (machine) in the traditional sense. A virtual machine emulates a physical machine but is not a real computer with its own hardware even though it can act as one. Here are some materials that I have found for you:

From http://www.serverwatch.com/server-trends/slideshows/top-10-virtualization-technology-companies-for-2016.html as of 06-09-2017

Top 10 Virtualization Technology Companies for 2016

VMware dominates the server virtualization market. Its domination doesn't stop with its commercial product, VMware vSphere. VMware also dominates the desktop-level virtualization market and perhaps even the free server virtualization market with its VMware Server product. VMware remains in the dominant spot due to its innovations, strategic partnerships and rock-solid products.

I agree. From discussions with other IT professionals I personally know and see frequently, VMware is at the top. One of them has been to multiple VM week-long conferences where thousands go annually.

Also from the same source:

> Microsoft came up with the only non-Linux hypervisor, Hyper-V, to compete in a tight server virtualization market that VMware currently dominates. Not easily outdone in the data center space, Microsoft offers attractive licensing for its Hyper-V product and the operating systems that live on it.
>
> For all Microsoft shops, Hyper-V is a viable solution that has only gotten more competitive in the virtualization space with each new Windows Server release. Microsoft has also been steadily gaining traction with enterprises looking to leverage the company's Azure cloud services as well as those interested in managing both on-premises Hyper-V services and Azure services.

Hyper-V has made inroads. Another of my IT professional contacts has used it widely while working for a Managed Service Provider (MSP) for its Small to Medium Business (SMB) clients. The most common place they are used in the SMB space is for clients who cannot afford to have much if any down time, for whom down time costs more than the cost of implementing and maintaining an infrastructure that uses virtualization. Examples of such environments are healthcare, financial services, and retail entities, just to name three.

And again from the same source:

> Citrix was once the lone wolf of application virtualization, but now it also owns the world's most-used cloud vendor software: Xen (the basis for its commercial XenServer). Amazon uses Xen for its Elastic Compute Cloud (EC2) services. So do Rackspace, Carpathia, SoftLayer and 1and1 for their cloud offerings. On the

corporate side, you're in good company with Bechtel, SAP and TESCO.

As you can see, numerous major companies and services use virtualization for servers and workstations. And for good reason. Virtual machines are useful in speed of recovery. They can also be the way a business operates on a day to day basis. One reason is that it can save a huge amount of investment in hardware. One computer hosting many virtual machines may need to be a more expensive unit than is typical for other scenarios, but since it is one vs. many, overall costs will be much lower. It goes even further. One unit vs. many means less electricity to run all the machines and less heat is generated. Less heat means lower cooling cost. And one unit vs. many means it takes up less space.

13 THE BACKUP PART OF RANSOMWARE PREVENTION AND RECOVERY

Regarding up-to-date backups, that alone may not afford the option of restoring to a point in time before an infection. Up-to-date implies just the most current version. But the most current version is the most likely to have the infection and is the most likely to be encrypted beyond use by ransomware. Being able to restore to a point in time before an infection involves backup planning and settings within very robust backup software. Those settings need to be tailored to what is being backed up. Static data, such as that of prior year archives, can have different settings than that made for data that changes daily. The settings may need to allow for a choice of retention and rollback based upon the number of days, the number of backups, the number of changes made to a file, or a date-based period.

In addition to well-configured backup, the location of and access method to the backup is also important. As stated at the front end of this book, ransomware commonly targets backup files. It is critical that at least one of your backup types include an offsite storage type of backup and that it be kept in a manner that is not connected to the systems that might get infected with ransomware. Legacy systems that meet these conditions include tapes that are picked up and stored off site. Modern systems that meet these conditions include offsite backup services such as the one I own called Backup Deposit Box.

David C. Pettit

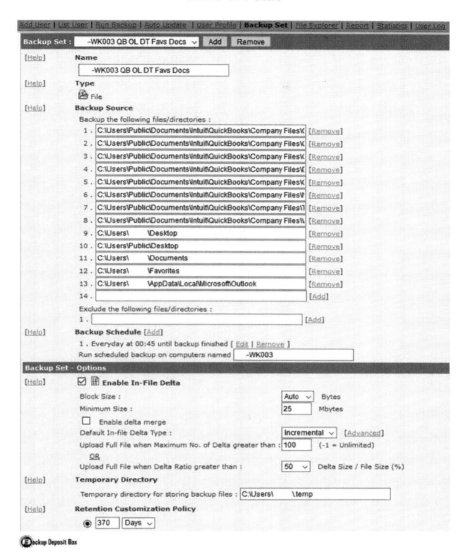

Note in the above image the bottom item – a Retention Customization Policy of 370 days. That is just over a year. The backed up files in that "Backup Set" give the company a long period for rolling back to a point before a ransomware attack or any other cause of data loss. There are even more relevant system and configuration settings that make that backup set resistant to complete compromise by ransomware.

14 THE BUSINESS END OF RANSOMWARE PREVENTION AND RECOVERY

Backup is only part of a disaster recovery plan for dealing with a ransomware attack. One prospective client signed up with my company after I performed a backup review with him, intending to perform a test restore using his then existing system. I could not find any backup files. I showed him that although his backup was installed and had some configuration settings made, no backups had run and none existed. He had for a long time had a false sense of security. Had he not had my review, he would have been very sad some months later when some of his original folders went missing. As it was, since he switched to my company after the review of his old backup system, recovery was fast and easy from the solution we had implemented for him. He later said "This saved my bacon." (Mel Ussing, CPA, Portland, Oregon.) The point is that having backup is one thing, while knowing for certain that data can be restored is yet another.

MELVIN E. USSING
CERTIFIED PUBLIC ACCOUNTANT

4506 SE BELMONT, SUITE 230 · PORTLAND, OREGON 97215-1658 · 503-230-7718 · 503-233-2685 FAX
E-MAIL _____@msn.com

November 10, 2009

The Info Tech Group LLC

Dear Dave:

I want to thank you for introducing me to your offsite backup service.

The first thing we found out was our tape back was not working and the system gave us no indication that it was not working.

It was not to long after we started using your service that we had a problem with a file on our server be damaged and with your help we were able to download from the offsite back the last version of that file and restore the file as save us a lot of time recreating the file and the information contained in it.

We have also had another occasion to use the offsite backup to restore a lost file.

I know for me the biggest and most important fact is that there is an offsite secure back up of all the data files on my serve, so incase of a major disaster such as fire or water damage to equipment that I have a recovery method in place.

I do recommend your service when ever I get a chance.

Thanks

Sincerely,

Melvin E Ussing

Adequate backup that can be restored is critical to recovery from a ransomware attack. But there is even more. Business continuity planning should include business level thought processes, not just technical things like backup and restore of files. How will the business function during and right after an attack? Risk Assessment should be performed in order to allow for budgeting and for the best possible defenses to be put in place. Incident Response should be planned out for when an attack happens in spite of good defenses. Alerting of staff and any other legally required and regulatory compliance notifications must be planned. Staff responsibilities need to be well understood and known. Correct reactions need to be decided upon ahead of time. Below I will provide you with materials for all of those.

Ransomware: Prevention and Recovery

15 ABOUT PAYING A RANSOM

Don't pay a ransom if you can help it.

From http://www.securityinfowatch.com/article/12337355/ransomware-the-risk-is-real 06-13-2017

Ransomware: The Risk is Real

Most security experts do not recommend supporting these terror organizations by paying them, as it leads to further risk of additional attacks and promotes the criminal mindset of the ransomware industry. But the fact is, without appropriate data backups, organizations are left with little choice.

Many don't recover their files even after paying a ransom. How does a 42% chance of recovery sound to you?

From https://heimdalsecurity.com/blog/what-is-ransomware-protection/ 06-13-2017

What is Ransomware and 15 Easy Steps To Keep Your System Protected [Updated]

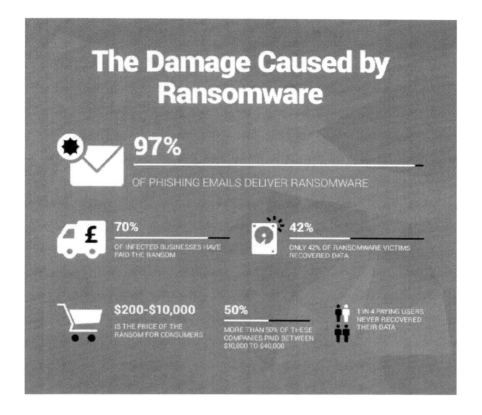

Finally, the option of paying the ransom remains. In terms of fiducial responsibility, a company decision maker might opt to pay the ransom if it is determined that the ransom is significantly less than the cost of another method of recovery and it is expected that such would be the end of the event. On the other hand, one might choose to never pay a ransom on principle. If a company considers it to be more of a financial decision than one of principle, then part of the plan for response and recovery may need to include preparation for making payment. One author of a big book on ransomware suggests that such preparation include having a Bitcoin account since payment by Bitcoin is a common requirement of the criminals. That approach is not for me and my company. But as an IT professional, I will support whatever my clients choose for themselves.

From https://en.wikipedia.org/wiki/Ransomware 06-12-2017

> A 2016 survey commissioned by Citrix claimed that larger businesses are holding bitcoin as contingency plans.

At a minimum, having an account and procedures for using it fast are one way to prepare for the option to make a ransom payment.

David C. Pettit

Or not!

Ransomware: Prevention and Recovery

16 MANAGED SECURITY SERVICES

Even if you do not have an arrangement with a Managed Services Provider (MSP) for all of your information technology needs, the minimum you need these days is a Managed Security Services agreement with a qualified information security company, team, or professional. Why do I say this? Because more than one online backup client of mine – clients in remote states who used their own local technology service companies as needed – failed to keep the backup up to date with changes made at the business. These were clients who handled their information technology in what the industry calls a "break/fix" manner. Let's pause and define that so you can understand how vulnerable a company can be without even realizing it. Here is a definition of both "break/fix" and "managed services" from Wikipedia.

From https://en.wikipedia.org/wiki/Break/fix 06-19-2017

The term break/fix refers to the fee-for-service method of providing information technology services to businesses. Using this method an IT solution provider performs services as needed and bills the customer only for the work done. The service may include repairs, upgrades or installation of systems, components, peripheral equipment, networking or software.

and

From https://en.wikipedia.org/wiki/Managed_services 06-09-2017

Managed services is the practice of outsourcing on a proactive basis management responsibilities and functions and a strategic method for improving operations and cutting expenses.

. . .

Adopting managed services is known to be an efficient way to stay up to date on technology, have access to necessary skills and address a range of issues related to cost, quality of service and risk.

The clients, who did not arrange for a managed services model for their information technology needs, could have and should have managed their own backup, but they didn't do it. They let their backup settings get so out of date that critical data that was lost had never been backed up. One lost more than a year of data. Ouch! Before that I was against managed services for companies in most industries, but not any longer. I now believe that all companies that do not have in-house full-time information technology staff need to, at a minimum, have their information security needs met with a Managed Security Services model of support from an outside company. That service should include those things that will protect and allow full, fast and inexpensive recovery from ransomware. Rip City IT Services, where I perform my work now, is a company that will create a custom plan to fit your company and budget. And if you don't need full managed services for all your information technology needs, you can arrange with Rip City IT Services for the most essential part of that, what they uniquely call Managed Security Services. They will learn your needs and then tailor a plan for your greatest return on your investment, making sure that you are not vulnerable to the loss of data. That will include loss from ransomware encryption as well as all the other forms of data loss for which backup is the solution. They service businesses with three to hundreds of computer systems. If that is you, give them a call.

Ransomware: Prevention and Recovery

17 ACTIONABLE ITEMS

Know where to begin so that you can reach the goal. You need at least some approved and published policies and procedures. Larger companies will need even more written documents. Regardless of company size, you will need to perform, or have performed for you, a risk assessment. If an attack occurs and if it applies to your industry, you may need to perform legally required notifications. Appropriate staff should sign up for security alerts. You will need to budget for prevention, any legally required notification costs, and recovery. You may wish to establish and fund a contingency fund. You will need to assign responsibilities for response, alerting, reacting, notifications, and recovery. If you don't have a full-time technology staff person to handle all of that for your company, then you need at least a Managed Security Services agreement, if not a full-on Managed Services agreement, with a qualified information technology services company.

Starting in Chapter 19 are some helpful standards, policies, procedures, checklists, forms, and guidelines. Each has sample parts for you to use as a starting point in making your own. You can get complete documents through Rip City IT Services at RipCityITServices.com

Ransomware: Prevention and Recovery

18 SECURITY ALERT SUGGESTIONS

Here are some security alert providers. I suggest you sign up with some. If you outsource your information technology security, then that entity needs to be the one getting the alerts.

Symantec offers a breaking news alert service for free.

From http://know.symantec.com/LP=1367 06-19-2017

> Symantec's Emergency Response System - Breaking News Alerts from Symantec
>
> Do you want to know when breaking news events -- including new vulnerabilities and malware outbreaks -- may impact your systems?
>
> Symantec, a leader in information security, offers a free email alert service through our Emergency Response System to help you protect your organization from newly discovered threats. Our security research centers around the world provide unparalleled analysis of and protection from IT security threats, such as malware,

zero-day vulnerabilities, and advanced cyberattacks. Bolster your organization's defenses and subscribe to our free email alert service today.

The US Department of Homeland Security offers an alert notification service. The page has a link that redirects one to another Internet domain, but that seems planned and seems to be safe.

From https://www.us-cert.gov/ncas/alerts 06-19-2017

Alerts

Alerts provide timely information about current security issues, vulnerabilities, and exploits. Sign up to receive these technical alerts in your inbox . . .

Below that is a large list of items. But to sign up for alerts, click on the "Sign up" link in the sentence above the list. When you do, your browser will redirect to another domain, govdelivery.com. See below.

From https://public.govdelivery.com/accounts/ USDHSUSCERT/subscriber/new 06-19-2017

You must enter a primary email address. You will use this to access and update your subscriptions or modify your subscriber preferences.

In spite of the above sentence, you will have the choice of alerts by email or by SMS / Text Message. The next page will give you some options. I recommend the following one:

Subscription Topics

National Cyber Awareness System Mailing Lists

Alerts

Click the check box and then click on the

Submit button at the bottom of the list.

Here is another one. Recorded Future offers daily cyber threat reports.

From https://go.recordedfuture.com/cyber-daily
06-19-2017

> Get Trending Threat Insights Delivered to Your Inbox With Our Free Cyber Daily
>
> Here is what one subscriber says about it: *"I look forward to the Cyber Daily update email every morning to start my day. It's timely and exact, with a quick overview of emerging threats and vulnerabilities."*
> Tom Doyle, Chief Information Officer, EBI Consulting'
>
> Just provide a business email and job function, click on the "Subscribe me" check box, and click the Subscribe button to get signed up.

Ransomware: Prevention and Recovery

19 RANSOMWARE STANDARDS

Here is a possible ransomware standard:

[ABC] Corporate Standard Regarding Ransomware and Other Malware

Our company will maximize the value of its information assets and reputation by using best practices to protect its information assets and mitigate any attack on its computer data.

(For companies with a need for regulatory compliance such as for the Health Insurance Portability and Accountability Act (HIPAA), Sarbanes Oxley (SOX), and the Gramm-Leach-Bliley Act (GLBA), more is needed. See an information security professional who has relevant materials. I have and will provide, to qualified prospective clients, a sample standard that includes appropriate terminology for compliance. You may use it as a template for creating your own standard.)

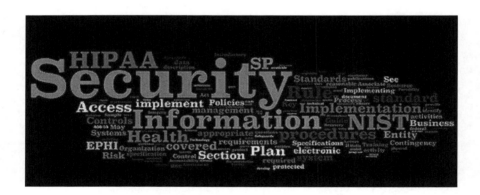

20 RANSOMWARE POLICIES

Here are two possible ransomware policy titles and one line item in each:

[ABC] Corporate Policy Regarding Ransomware and Other Malware

All staff must immediately stop all computer mouse and keyboard activity upon suspicion or evidence of a malware or ransomware attempt, attack, or infection, and promptly notify the company designated information technology (IT) service vendor contact, or, if the company IT service vendor contact is not

immediately available, call the support line of our company IT service vendor and report the incident with as much detail as possible.

An example line item in a policy for a company's IT service vendor is:

[ABC] Corporate Policy for IT Service Vendors

Upon suspicion or evidence of a malware or ransomware attempt, attack, or infection, the IT service company will immediately arrange to isolate all company computer systems and cut off the company connection to the Internet for the purpose of minimizing the spread of the infection and the chance of infected systems contacting the malware's "headquarters" for encryption keys or to pass sensitive information. The IT service vendor will keep originals or copies of infected systems and files for the purposes of investigation, prosecution, and perhaps eventual decryption should a decryption solution be needed and be forthcoming. The IT service company will log and track all remediation and

recovery activity and provide hourly verbal status reports to our company point of contact, or, if such contact is not immediately available, any designated substitute.

Of course there is much more that needs to be included for either policy. I can provide to you, a qualified prospective client, sample policies that may be used as templates for creating your own policies.

21 RANSOMWARE PROCEDURES

Here are two possible ransomware procedures titles, each with one sample line item. The first is for a corporation with an internal IT department and is about user-owned devices. The second is for a company that has no full time internal IT staff and is about incident response.

IT Department Ransomware Procedures

All Bring Your Own Device (BYOD) equipment must be screened before it may connect in any way to any company service or system.

Ransomware Incident Response Procedures

Staff who suspect, notice, or discover ransomware exposure or an attack must do the following:

1) Stop all computer mouse and keyboard activity
2) Notify the company single point of contact to the company information technology (IT) service vendor or else, if the single point of contact is not immediately available, immediately call the support line of our company IT service vendor and report the incident with as much detail as possible.
3) If directed to do so, notify all other staff – those who are on premise as well as those who are off premise – that 1) a malware attack may be under way, 2) that appropriate notification has been made, 3) all computer and other connected devices may experience some disruption as they are isolated and the Internet connection is disabled, and 4) the company IT

services vendor will notify the company when normal computer operations may resume.

Staff who receive notification that an attack may be in progress and who have devices that are not actively connected to the company network must not connect again to the network until given the go ahead by the designated IT point of contact or by a staff person of our company IT services vendor.

Ransomware: Prevention and Recovery

22 RANSOMWARE CHECKLISTS

Ransomware Risk Assessment Checklist

Here are some of the things that need to be included on a Risk Assessment Checklist:

- ☐ Firewall settings review
- ☐ Router configuration review
- ☐ Server protection review
- ☐ Endpoint (workstation, laptop) protection review
- ☐ Mobile devices review (phones, tablets, etc.)

Ransomware: Prevention and Recovery

IT Department Ransomware Protection Checklist

Here are some items to include on an IT Department Ransomware Protection Checklist

- ☐ Disable workstation browsers unless necessary for the tasks performed by the role of the staff person

- ☐ Limit domain logon accounts to the lowest account level possible for the tasks performed by the role of the staff person, and, under no circumstances, allow any non-IT staff person's domain account to have Administrative Privileges

- ☐ Give your system admins secondary accounts and do not allow them to use administrative accounts for day-to-day non-admin work; they can use elevated permissions for certain processes as needed from those more limited accounts

- ☐ Install chosen detection and protection software on all

network-connected devices

☐ **Scan everything everywhere all the time (this is in regard to live user email and Internet web activity; do not scan all files on all file storage all the time, but rather on a regular and frequent basis after work hours)**

☐ **Log all network traffic**

David C. Pettit

IT Department Ransomware Response Checklist

Demisto has good material for incident response to a ransomware attack.

From https://www.demisto.com/playbook-for-handling-ransomware-infections/ 06-20-2017

> The main goal is to contain, eradicate and recover from the infections as soon as possible.

The following could be part of your company's IT Department Ransomware Response Checklist

- ☐ Isolate a victimized unit
- ☐ Cut off connectivity to the Internet, at least until victimized devices are isolated from the network
- ☐ Open a support ticket and begin the entries for the incident with Who What When Where and with the fact of the isolation of the unit (s) and the cut-off of Internet connectivity

Ransomware: Prevention and Recovery

- **Determine if the attack is real or a false positive; if a false positive, reconnect the network to the Internet and remove the reported unit from isolation**

- **Discover all victimized devices**

- **Determine how the victim's device was infected**

- **(the complete checklist will be very long, yet, in spite of that, response to a ransomware attack must be adaptable and so do not reply only on this checklist; instead, adapt and add to it whatever seems appropriate for the incident)**

David C. Pettit

Ransomware IT Department Recovery Checklist

Here are some of the things that need to be included on a Ransomware IT Department Recovery Checklist:

- ☐ Provide the affected staff with replacement computers, devices, or virtual machines (if using such technology)

- ☐ Scan any affected servers and either repair or replace the servers

- ☐ Scan and remove any infected files from file storage devices and drives

- ☐ Restore files as needed

- ☐ (the complete checklist will be very custom for your company information technology environment)

The above are just examples. Consider having and using even more checklists.

23 RANSOMWARE FORMS

The following are just some examples with partial content. You will most likely need to have more forms than these. You will certainly need more content in them. Because a ransomware attack is just one of many types of problems or disasters, you may just cover in these ransomware forms some of the same as you would in your other disaster recovery plan (DRP) forms, or provide a summary and then refer to those.

Ransomware Assigned Responsibilities Form

Recovery Lead/Coordinator

Disaster Recovery Coordinator – Responsible for the successful execution of the Disaster Recovery Plan. The individual coordinates actions of all Recovery Teams. This individual will likely be a member of a company IT Security team if one exists, otherwise will likely be a member of the IT team. If no full-time IT staff exist in the company, then this responsibility falls to the technology services vendor hired by the company.

Assessment and Replacement

Information Technology (IT) is responsible for the assessment of damaged computer equipment (e.g., servers, PCs, etc.), and subsequent repair or replacement of such equipment and for assessment of lost data, recovery of data from backup, and systems and data validation after recovery.

Ransomware Budget for Prevention, Notification, and Recovery Form

Ransomware Prevention Budget

    Firewall   _____

    Network Software   _____

    Endpoint Software   _____

    User Education   _____

    Consultants   _____

Ransomware Notification Budget

    Intercom system   _____

    Automated notification service subscription   _____

        (Think rapidreach.com, rapidnotify.com)

Ransomware Recovery Budget

    Spare servers   _____

    Spare workstations   _____

Having standards, policies, procedures, checklists, forms, and guidelines are one thing.

Knowing they will work is another. Proper preparation involves testing. Test all that may matter, especially checklists. Review forms more than once per year, especially the Assigned Responsibilities form, since staff changes happen frequently.

24 YOUR WORKSHEETS

Why wait? I recommend you begin to create your own standards, policies, procedures, forms, and guidelines right now and keep working at getting your company ready before ransomware hits. If you don't want to do it yourself, consider hiring Rip City IT Services to do it for you. Because they already have dozens of forms that just need customizing to your needs, you will likely save time, money, and omissions over doing them yourself or having another vendor do this work for you. Even if you choose to outsource this work, begin filling in the following so that you can provide your input to your chosen vendor company.

Ransomware: Prevention and Recovery

MY RANSOMWARE STANDARD 1

David C. Pettit

MY RANSOMWARE STANDARD 2

MY RANSOMWARE STANDARD 3

David C. Pettit

MY RANSOMWARE POLICY 1

MY RANSOMWARE POLICY 2

David C. Pettit

MY RANSOMWARE POLICY 3

MY RANSOMWARE PROCEDURE 1

David C. Pettit

MY RANSOMWARE PROCEDURE 2

MY RANSOMWARE PROCEDURE 3

David C. Pettit

MY RANSOMWARE CHECKLIST 1

MY RANSOMWARE CHECKLIST 2

David C. Pettit

MY RANSOMWARE CHECKLIST 3

MY RANSOMWARE FORMS 1

David C. Pettit

MY RANSOMWARE FORMS 2

MY RANSOMWARE FORMS 3

David C. Pettit

MY RANSOMWARE GUIDELINES 1

MY RANSOMWARE GUIDELINES 2

David C. Pettit

MY RANSOMWARE GUIDELINES 3

Ransomware: Prevention and Recovery

EPILOGUE

Before even getting this published, I saw the first result of a person reading this book, and it was positive. My wife, a non-technical person, let me know that she had just updated her smart phone even though she usually puts it off and rarely does so. This is a change of habit for her and is better for information and device security. Well done.

May I suggest that you share this book with another person when you are done reading it?

Ransomware: Prevention and Recovery

ABOUT THE AUTHOR

David Pettit owns an information technology support company and an online backup business. His more than 34 years full time in the technology industry and more than ten years full time in the online backup industry helps him give to you a perspective on ransomware that you will find very useful. He has studied for and passed over 30 certification exams and has had many certifications, including the following in information security: CISSP 2004-2007 and 2007-2010, MCSE: Security, MCSA: Security, and CompTIA Security+

He and his wife live in what they call the Deer Retreat – where deer come to eat apples and graze on leaves right next to their backyard.

Although they are empty-nesters, there seems to always be a Dachshund under foot, and the house and grounds are all decorated with Doxie decorations.

Ransomware: Prevention and Recovery

ENGAGEMENTS

David Pettit is available for speaking engagements about ransomware, information security, disaster recovery and business continuity, or cloud services. You may reach him through RipCityITServices.com

Made in the USA
Columbia, SC
30 June 2017